The Christian in Today's Society

LIVING
BIBLE
STUDIES in
Thessalonians

JOHN C. SOUTER

Tyndale House
Publishers, Inc.
Wheaton, Illinois
Coverdale House
Publishers, Ltd.
Eastbourne, England

Library of Congress
Catalog Card Number
76-47302
ISBN 0-8423-0238-7, paper

First printing
January 1977
Printed in the
United States of America

CONTENTS

INTRODUCTION *Page 9*

BACKGROUND *Page 13*

READY-REFERENCE SECTION *Page 17*

WEEK

1 **They Shook the World**
Acts 17:1-10 *Page 19*

2 **The Christian Life: Past, Present, and Future**
1 Thessalonians 1:1-10 *Page 29*

3 **The Soul Winner's Character**
1 Thessalonians 2:1-16 *Page 41*

4 **The Rewards of Being a Witness**
1 Thessalonians 2:17—3:13 *Page 53*

5 **The Pure Life**
1 Thessalonians 4:1-8 *Page 65*

6 **How to Mind Your Own Business**
1 Thessalonians 4:9-12 *Page 77*

7 **Future Tense—He's Coming Soon!**
1 Thessalonians 4:13-18 *Page 87*

8 **Wanted: Dead or Alive**
1 Thessalonians 5:1-11 *Page 99*

9 **Present Tense—Live the Christian Life with Power**
1 Thessalonians 5:12-28 *Page 111*

10 **Persecution? Here's What to Expect**
2 Thessalonians 1:1-12 *Page 123*

11 **The Man of Lawlessness**
2 Thessalonians 2:1-12 *Page 135*

12 **The Growth Experience**
2 Thessalonians 2:13—3:5 *Page 147*

13 **The Disciplined Life**
2 Thessalonians 3:6-18 *Page 159*

APPLICATION SUMMARY *Page 171*

INTRODUCTION

Attend a Bible study today, and almost certainly several in the group will have brought along their copies of *The Living Bible.* So many millions of this unique book have been purchased that recently it captured about half of the entire Bible sales in the United States. Have you ever wondered what makes this Bible so popular?

The Living Bible is a paraphrase. Instead of being a translation (like most other Bibles), it tries to expose the meaning of the original text by putting it into contemporary language. It reads like a best-selling novel and holds your interest as if the apostles and prophets were sitting in your living room.

The Living Bible has tremendous impact. The reader understands what he is reading. He finds himself becoming indignant at the callousness and sin of some Bible characters. He begins to weep with those who were weeping. He becomes involved in the life and teachings of Jesus. In short, he "lives" what he is reading.

This book is based on Kenneth Taylor's vibrant paraphrase. It is one in a series of Living Bible Studies designed to challenge your Christian life and make it a joyful experience.

The Christian Life: Past, Present, and Future

In all the Bible, few books contain as much interesting information as Paul's first and second letters to the Christians at Thessalonica. In these two dynamic books, Paul analyzes the past and shows us how to grow a spiritual church. He looks at the present and lays out principles of Christlike living. He predicts the future and tells us of the coming "rapture" of the church and the appearance of the Antichrist.

Here is a challenging study for young Christians. Whether you dig into God's Word on your own or in a study group, you will find *The Christian in Today's Society* an exciting adventure.

How to Use This Notebook

A few years ago, teachers in the public school system realized that a student learns more effectively and enjoys his classroom experience more fully if he discovers new facts by himself. Teachers soon began to use a variety of "discovery techniques" so a student could teach himself.

It is more enjoyable to discover Bible truths than it is to have them handed to you. This notebook is designed to help you discover on your own what the Word of God is saying. Many of the questions and learning experiences contained in *The Christian in Today's Society* are general (as opposed to specific questions that ask for specific answers). This has been done to make you think and discover for yourself.

With this notebook you will study the Bible every day for thirteen weeks. There are twenty-five different Bible study methods for you to use—some of them are simple and others are more complex. Each method will need between five and twenty-five minutes to complete.

If you are studying with a group, you will want to start (Week 1, Day 1) on the day your group first meets. In most chapters, Day 7 will give you a look at the passage you will be examining at the next study session.

During the week, as you complete each method, questions will arise. Jot these questions down at the end of the chapter under "Questions" so that you can quiz your Bible study group. When the study group leader brings out interesting information, you can record this information on the same page, under "Notes."

Set a definite time to study each day. Make this a high priority in your daily routine. Dawn is one of the best times for most people, as the early hours offer a quiet atmosphere and the mind is usually uncluttered. Morning Bible study is an excellent way to begin the day.

Choose a place where there will be no interruptions. It is wise to inform your family of this appointment with God's Word so they will respect this time. The phone may also have to be taken off the hook to avoid interruptions.

Avoid studying when your mind is tired or occupied with other things. If you aren't fresh and alert, you will have difficulty concentrating.

Don't allow yourself too much time. Set a deadline for completion of the study, and then gear your study to meet it. You will probably go past this completion time as you become absorbed in the passage, but the deadline will keep you working hard.

Any change in schedule will affect your Bible study time. Vacations, sickness, and days when your routine varies—for instance, on weekends—will tend to break your regularity. When such changes appear, reaffirm to yourself that nothing will take you away from God's Word.

The Importance of Application

Applying the principles of Scripture is essential to growth. "If a person just listens and doesn't obey, he is like a man looking at his face in a mirror; as soon as he walks away, he can't see himself anymore or remember what he looks like. But if anyone keeps looking steadily into God's law for free men, he will not only remember it but he will do what it says, and God will greatly bless him in everything he does" (James 1:23-25).

The Bible is a practical book. God wants to use it to change your character. If you don't apply his words, they become meaningless.

Scripture can reveal the thoughts and intentions of your heart. When you study the Bible, you may discover that some of your behavior and attitudes are inconsistent with God's will. The Bible will also point out new attitudes that you must form. An Application Summary has been provided at the back of this book so that you can transfer all your personal applications to one section. In this way you can continue to refer to them.

The World of the Thessalonian Church

About the time the Apostle Paul was beginning his first major missionary journey, the Roman emperor Gaius was suddenly murdered. Claudius, his fifty-year-old nephew, cowered behind the curtains in the palace to escape the killers. The Praetorian Guard discovered his hiding place, and because he was the only surviving member of the royal family, they promptly made him their new, if unwilling, emperor.

Because Roman military legions had control of the entire civilized world, events in the capital affected almost everyone. Although the new emperor was an unlikely choice for his office, he was not a tyrannical ruler.

Claudius received little public exposure before inheriting the throne; his mother and grandmother had considered him a little crazy. He was probably an epileptic who both stuttered and slobbered. Although his armies attacked and conquered part of Britain, his reign was generally marked with peace.

Claudius was in power when the Apostle and his companions reached 350-year-old Thessalonica. It had become the capital and largest city of Macedonia by the time these Christian missionaries arrived.

Because Rome's power was based on its invincible army, the empire was crisscrossed with a network of paved roads. These military arteries were well-constructed, carefully maintained, and reasonably safe. Thessalonica was located on the Egnatian Way, one of the military highways. The missionaries traveled this road to reach the city.

Not only was the city on an important road, it was situated at a key shipping location on the Aegean Sea, and therefore possessed a large population composed mostly of Greeks, with a few Romans, Asians, and Jews. Latin was the legal language of the empire, but in the east, Greek was the common tongue.

The houses in Thessalonica were probably constructed of stucco and sun-dried brick. Roofs were usually tile or thatch. Few homes had windows opening on the street because of the probability of theft. Large cities often had streets paved with marble and some had complete systems of night lighting. Underground sewer systems and public baths were also found in the major cities of the empire.

In pagan society aristocratic landowners, wealthy businessmen, and royalty lived in luxury. A strong middle class did not exist, but there was an abundance of slaves. Farmers, small businessmen, and artisans composed most of the free population.

Slaves may have outnumbered the freemen. Many slaves—the doctors, accountants, teachers, and copyists—were more educated than their masters. Paul's letters indicate there were slaves in Christian households and that many had become believers.

Immorality was common in pagan temples. Prostitution was a well-organized institution. Obscene pictures were often painted on the outside walls of houses. Infants, especially girls, were often abandoned by their parents. Divorce was easy and socially acceptable. Murders were frequent.

The Christians Come

Into this world the Apostle Paul came on his second missionary journey. Landing in Macedonia, he went immediately to the important city of Philippi. After founding a church and receiving considerable persecution, he and his small party traveled west on the Egnatian Way to Thessalonica.

The apostle's strategy was to plant churches at key geographical locations on the major trade routes. These churches served as bases for evangelizing the surrounding countryside.

Silas, Timothy, and Luke were Paul's main companions in this missionary thrust. Luke must have remained in Philippi for he is not mentioned again. After the apostles founded the church in Thessalonica, persecution by the Jews forced them to move on to Beroea. After more trouble erupted in Beroea, Paul traveled down to Athens alone.

Paul instructed Timothy and Silas to come to him as soon as possible. Apparently when Timothy arrived, Paul sent him back up to visit the Thessalonian church. When Paul continued farther south to Corinth, both Timothy and Silas joined him there.

Paul was in Corinth for eighteen months before Gallio, proconsul or governor of Achaia, assumed office (Acts 18:11, 12). We know from secular sources that this was in A.D. 51, so Paul was probably in Thessalonica somewhere around A.D. 48 or 49. The Apostle probably wrote both of his letters to the Thessalonian church from Corinth in the middle of A.D. 50.

Occasion for the Letters

In his first letter to the Thessalonian church, Paul shows that he had been concerned about the stability of their faith (3:5) after he left. When Timothy returned to the apostle with encouraging news about the church's growth, he must have brought with him several questions that the young group of believers wanted answered.

Throughout the first three chapters of this letter, the apostle defends his ministry, as if to answer the charges of his Jewish opponents. He praises the believers for standing up to persecution by their countrymen (2:14). He discusses events leading up to the coming of Christ for all Christians (4:14-18) and indicates how it will take place (5:1-11) to aid those who had forgotten his previous teachings on the subject.

Tension may have developed between some of the leading members of the congregation and the rest of the believers (5:12, 13), as Paul touches on the subject of esteeming spiritual leaders. He also deals with those who were content to live off their Christian friends instead of earning their own living (4:11, 12).

Second Thessalonians was undoubtedly written several months after the first letter in response to a report that the problems were still not solved.

The defense of his own conduct had apparently been successful, because he does not repeat it. However, the undisciplined conduct must have continued (3:6-15) as well as questioning about the Lord's coming (2:1-12). Paul also stresses how pleased he is with the church's perseverance under heavy persecution (1:1-10). In the second letter he attempts to put things in order within the church.

Apostle Paul. Name means "little" (originally named Saul which means "asked for").
Paul's education. Phil. 3:5; 22:3; 23:6; 26:4, 5; Gal. 1:14.
Citizenship. Acts 16:37-39; 22:25-28.
Persecution of Christians. Acts 7:57—8:3; 9:1, 2; 22:4, 5; 26:9-11; 1 Tim. 1:13.
Conversion. Acts 9:1-20; 22:3-21; 26:2-23.
Early Christian life. Acts 9:17-30; 11:22-30; Gal. 1:15-20.
First missionary journey. Acts 13:1—14:28; Gal. 1:21-24.
Second missionary journey. Acts 15:36—18:22.
Third missionary journey. Acts 18:23—21:16.
Trial and imprisonment at Rome. Acts 21:17—28:31.

Silas or Silvanus. Names mean "asked."
Sent to Paul. Acts 15:22.
His spiritual gift. Acts 15:32 (see *TLB* footnote).
Becomes Paul's companion. Acts 15:40, 41; 1 Thes. 1:1; 2 Thes. 1:1.
Imprisoned with Paul at Philippi. Acts 16:1-40.
Driven from Thessalonica with Paul. Acts 17:1-10.
Left at Beroea. Acts 17:11-14.
Rejoins Paul. Acts 17:15; 18:5.
Carries Peter's epistle to Asia. 1 Pet. 5:12.

Timothy or Timotheus. Names mean "honoring God."
Family background. Acts 16:1-3; 2 Tim. 1:5, 6
Temperament. 1 Cor. 16:10, 11; 2 Tim. 1:4, 7, 8.
Paul's spiritual child. 1 Tim. 1:2; 2 Tim. 1:2; 1 Cor. 4:17.
Possessed a spiritual gift. 1 Tim. 4:14; 2 Tim. 1:6.
Physical ailments. 1 Tim. 5:23.
Paul's confidence. Phil. 2:19-22; 1 Cor. 4:17.
Participation in second missionary journey. Acts 16:1—18:17; 2 Cor. 1:19; 1 Thes. 3:1, 2.
Left in Beroea. Acts 17:14, 15.
Sent to Thessalonica. 1 Thes. 3:2, 6.
Rejoins Paul at Corinth. Acts 18:5.
Participated in third missionary journey. Acts 19:21, 22; 1 Cor. 4:17; 16:10; 2 Cor. 1:1.

With Paul in Rome. Phil. 2:19; Col. 1:1; Philem. 1:1.
Paul writes him twice from second Roman imprisonment. 1 and 2 Tim.

Thessalonian Converts

Demas. Col. 4:14; Philem. 24; 2 Tim. 4:10.
Gaius. Acts 19:29.
Secundus. Acts 20:4.
Aristarchus. Acts 19:29; 20:4; 27:2; Col. 4:10.
Jason. Acts 17:4-9.

Subjects in Thessalonian Epistles

Morality. 1 Thes. 4:3-8; 1 Cor. 6:8, 9, 13-20; 2 Cor. 12:20, 21; Heb. 13:4; Matt. 5:27, 28.
Antichrist. 2 Thes. 2:3-11; Dan. 7:8, 20-26; Rev. 13:1-8.
Rapture. 1 Thes. 4:15-17; 2 Thes. 2:1; Acts 1:9-11; 1 Cor. 15:51-53; Matt. 24:40-44; Luke 17:30-37.
Day of the Lord. 1 Thes. 5:2-4; 2 Thes. 2:2; Acts 2:20; 2 Pet. 3:10; Isa. 2:12; Joel 1:15; Amos 5:18.
Work habits. 1 Thes. 4:11, 12; 2 Thes. 3:6-15; Eph. 4:28; Acts 20:34; 2:44; 1 Tim. 5:13; Col. 3:23, 24.
Death. 1 Thes. 4:13-16; Phil. 1:20-24; Heb. 9:27; 2 Cor. 5:8-10; Rev. 20:14; Rom. 6:23.

They Shook the World
ACTS 17:1-10

WEEK

1

Introduction

The first visit of Paul, Silas, and Timothy to Thessalonica (Acts 17) shows us successful men in action. Every ingredient necessary for success can be found in their lives. They had a dynamic message which they presented with force. They were confident, organized, knowledgeable, and sensitive to needs. They were ready to suffer anything, to pay any price to reach the city with the message of Christ.

People are attracted to "winners." It shouldn't surprise us that the apostles, who arrived with a world-shaking reputation, left only when they had turned Thessalonica upside down. Examine carefully this work which they started. Be alert as you read the two letters Paul wrote to this group of believers and discover how to live the Christian life more fully.

WEEK 1/ DAY 1 **Verse Glance** Date ______

Look up Hebrews 4:12.

1 What is the subject of the verse?

______

______

2 What phrases are used to describe the subject?

______

______

3 What is the purpose of this verse?

______

______

4 What does this verse say to you?

______

______

WEEK 1/ DAY 2 Date ____________

Five W's / Who, When, Where, What, Why

Skim Acts 17:1-9.

1 *Who* were involved?

2 *When* did this event take place?

APPROXIMATE DATE

DAY OF WEEK

RELATIONSHIP TO OTHER EVENTS

3 *Where* did the action take place?

EMPIRE

PROVINCE

CITY

GEOGRAPHY

BUILDING

4 *What* took place?

5 *Why* did this event take place?

6 What is God teaching you in this passage?

WEEK 1/ DAY 3 **Observation** Date ____________

Read Acts 17:10-15 carefully.

1 Why did the brethren send Paul and Silas away?

2 Why did Paul go to the Jews first? (Acts 17:1, 2)

3 Who was more open-minded than the Thessalonian Jews?

4 What did these people do to reveal their openmindedness?

5 What can you learn from the Beroeans about your attitude toward Scripture?

6 Was Paul right in fleeing from the Thessalonian Jews? Should he have remained?

7 Is it better for modern-day Christians to share their faith by example rather than open proclamation? (If we proclaim, we may also offend.)

WEEK 1/ DAY 4 **Teachings of Jesus** Date ____________

Read Luke 9:2-5 carefully.

1 What did Jesus command?

2 What did Jesus condemn?

3 What good qualities was he encouraging?

4 Why did Jesus give this command?

5 What is the underlying principle he was teaching?

6 How can you apply these teachings?

WEEK 1/ DAY 5 **Book Study, Part 1** Date ____________
Skim 1 Thessalonians.

BACKGROUND (use Ready-Reference if necessary)

1 Who was the writer?

____

____

OCCUPATION

____

APPROXIMATE AGE

____

PERSONALITY TRAITS

2 Where was the book written?

____

3 Where was it sent?

____

4 When was it written?

____

5 Why was it written?

____

____

THEME

1 What ideas stand out at your first reading?

____

____

____

2 Summarize the contents of the book.

____

____

____

3 What verses stand out?

____

WEEK 1/ DAY 6 **Book Study, Part 2** Date ____________

Read 1 Thessalonians quickly.

SPECIAL CHARACTERISTICS

1 What are some of the important teachings of this book?

____

____

____

2 What personal information does the author give?

____

____

____

OUTLINE SUMMARY

Write out a simple outline of the main points contained in the book.

____

____

____

____

____

____

____

____

____

____

APPLICATION

What subjects does this book deal with that you personally need?

____

____

____

WEEK 1/ DAY 7 **Meditation** Date ____________

Read 1 Thessalonians 1:1-10, considering the meaning of each phrase.

1 Choose a verse to meditate on today. Rephrase it in your own words.

2 What has God taught you from this passage?

Notes

Questions

The Christian Life: Past, Present, and Future

1 THESSALONIANS 1:1-10

WEEK 2

Introduction

Here is Paul's first New Testament letter. The Apostle reveals the power of dynamic Christian living in chapter one. The world was fast becoming aware of Christianity, not only by Paul's ministry, but by the witness of the vibrant Thessalonian believers. What had happened to these ordinary people to transform them into powerful propagators of the faith?

Paul outlines their Christian experience: past, present, and future. He explains how the Macedonians had believed in Christ, how they had become faithful witnesses, and what the result of their faith would bring in the future. As you study the Christian life of these new converts, examine your own personal walk with the Lord.

Outline

1 Thessalonians 1:1-10

I Introduction of the letter (1:1)
II The state of the church (1:2-10)
  A. The importance of prayer to the church (1:2)
  B. The character of the church (1:3)
  C. The good news comes to the church (1:4-6)
    1. The church was chosen by God (1:4)
    2. Presentation of the good news (1:5)
    3. Reception of the good news (1:6)
  D. The reputation of the church (1:7-10)
    1. You became an example (1:7)
    2. You spread the Word everywhere (1:8)
    3. Your testimony keeps coming back to us (1:9)
    4. You are waiting for the Lord's return (1:10)

WEEK 2/ DAY 1 **Tense Study** Date ____________

Look carefully at 1 Thessalonians 1:1-10.

Put each verse in the passage into the proper column below. Did it happen in the past? Is it still happening? Will it happen in the future?

PAST	PRESENT	FUTURE

1 *Past:* What are some of your benefits from the past?

____

____

2 *Present:* What should you be doing now?

____

____

3 *Future:* What does the future hold?

____

____

WEEK 2/ DAY 2 **Epistle Study** Date ____________
Review quickly 1 Thessalonians 1:1-6.

1 Check the type(s) of passage. (You may feel that the passage fits more than one category.)
Doctrinal ____ Instructional ____ Personal ____
Correctional ____

2 What personal information does the author give?

____

____

____

3 What kind of example does the apostle live?

____

____

____

4 What part did the Holy Spirit take in Paul's ministry?

____

____

____

____

5 What are the important elements of the presentation of the gospel?

____

____

____

6 What basic principles is God teaching you in this passage?

____

____

____

____

WEEK 2/ DAY 3 **Epistle Study** Date ____________
Review quickly 1 Thessalonians 1:7-10.

1 Check the type(s) of passage:
Doctrinal ____ Instructional ____ Personal ____
Correctional ____

2 What personal information does the author give?

____

____

____

3 What information is given about the Thessalonians?

____

____

____

____

4 What proof did the apostle have that the Thessalonians were Christians?

____

____

____

____

5 What doctrinal truths are given concerning Christ?

____

____

____

____

6 What principles is God teaching you in this passage?

____

____

____

WEEK 2/ DAY 4 **Contrast** Date ___________
Read Hebrews 13:7, 17; Philippians 3:17; 2 Timothy 2:2.

1 What responsibility do we as Christians have toward our spiritual leaders?

____

____

2 Should we still obey our spiritual leaders when they appear to be wrong?

____

____

____

3 What spiritual leaders are you subject to?

____

4 Are you disciplining anyone? Who looks to you as a spiritual leader?

____

Thessalonica Today

Thessalonica still survives as a city. Today it is called Salonika and is one of the largest cities in Greece. Unlike Philippi and Corinth whose sites were later abandoned, modern Salonika has been built on the remains of the ancient city so that almost no ruins remain.

What happened to the thriving Christian church the apostle established in the city? There is little doubt that the present-day Greek Orthodox Church, which claims 97 percent of the country's population, can trace its history back to first-century Christianity, though the actual church that Paul founded no longer exists. The Greek Orthodox Church is a far cry from the vibrant evangelical community that lived in that city 1,900 years ago.

Yet the church Paul founded did not really die. The Word of God is still spreading from the spiritual descendants of those early Thessalonian believers—and it will continue to spread until the Lord returns.

 Newspaper Report Date ____________

1 Write a newspaper article for the local Thessalonian press. Write from a secular point of view using Acts 17:1-10 and 1 Thes. 1:1-10 for your facts.

2 The introduction to your article should include *who* was involved, *when* the events took place, *where* they happened, and *what* happened (see Five W's, Week 1, Day 2).

3 The rest of your article should contain *how* and *why* and any additional facts.

THESSALONICA (UPI)—____________________________

WEEK 2/ DAY 6 **Grammar Study** Date ___________

Look up 1 Thessalonians 1:3.

1 What is the subject of the sentence?

____

2 What is the subject doing?

____

3 What is Paul doing (see verse 2)?

____

4 What are the three things that Paul didn't want to forget?

____

____

____

5 What qualities of character should you pursue?

____

____

____

WEEK 2/ DAY 7 **Meditation** Date ____________

Read 1 Thessalonians 2:1-16, considering the meaning of each phrase.

1 Choose a verse to meditate on today. Rephrase it in your own words.

2 What has God taught you from this passage?

Notes

Questions

The Soul Winner's Character

1 THESSALONIANS 2:1-16

WEEK

3

Introduction

In chapter two, Paul describes the kind of behavior a soul winner should exhibit. This greatest of all missionaries uses his own evangelistic team as an example.

As he reviews the opposition of the past, he reveals that he and his companions were bold. Their gospel presentation didn't spring from error, impurity, greed, or the desire for human praise. They didn't flatter people or throw their weight around. They worked hard to support themselves financially and presented Christ with tender love and affection.

These men of God lived a model of the type of character a soul winner should exhibit. We would do well to pattern our personal witness after them.

Outline

1 Thessalonians 2:1-16

III Relations of the apostles to the church (2:1—3:13)
- A. Their conduct toward the church (2:1-12)
  1. Paul reminds the church of the persecution they received (2:1-3)
     - a. You knew how we had been persecuted (2:1, 2)
     - b. You knew our motives were pure (2:3)
  2. Paul defends their ministry (2:4-12)
     - a. We did not warp God's message (2:4)
     - b. We did not try to win you with flattery (2:5)
     - c. We never asked for praise (2:6)
     - d. We treated you gently with love (2:7, 8)
     - e. We worked hard not to be a burden (2:9)
     - f. We behaved faultlessly toward you (2:10)
     - g. We pleaded that your daily lives should not embarrass God (2:11, 12)
- B. Paul praises the church's response to the Good News (2:13)
- C. Paul condemns the persecutors (2:14-16)
  1. You suffered persecution like the Judean believers (2:14)
  2. The Jews persecuted the Judeans (2:15, 16)

WEEK 3/ DAY 1 **Paragraph Glance** Date ____________

Summarize the contents of each paragraph division of 1 Thessalonians listed below. Be as brief as possible.

REFERENCE	SUMMARY
1:1	
1:2, 3	
1:4-6	
1:7-10	
2:1-3	
2:4-8	
2:9-12	
2:13	
2:14-16	
2:17-20	
3:1-4	
3:5-8	
3:9-13	
4:1-5	
4:6-8	
4:9-12	
4:13-14	
4:15-18	
5:1-3	
5:4-8	
5:9-11	
5:12-13	
5:14-18	
5:19-28	

WEEK 3/ DAY 2 **Epistle Study** Date ____________
Review quickly 1 Thessalonians 2:1-12.

1 Check the type(s) of passage:
Doctrinal____ Instructional____ Personal____
Correctional____

2 Summarize the personal information the author gives:

____

____

3 What problem was the apostle trying to correct?

____

____

____

4 What does Paul point out to defend his Thessalonian ministry?

____

____

____

5 In what ways did the apostles show their love and concern?

____

____

6 What basic doctrinal truths can you glean from this passage?

____

____

____

7 What principles does God want you to learn?

____

____

____

WEEK 3/ DAY 3 **Epistle Study** Date ____________
Review quickly 1 Thessalonians 2:13-16.

1 Check the type(s) of passage:
Doctrinal____ Instructional____ Personal____
Correctional____

2 Summarize the personal information given in this section.

____

____

3 What light does the context throw on the passage?

____

____

4 Describe the behavior of non-Christian Jews toward the gospel.

____

____

5 Why did these Jews react so hostilely to the gospel? Why was Paul so hostile before his conversion?

____

____

____

6 What basic doctrinal truths can you glean from this passage?

____

____

____

____

7 What principles does God want you to learn?

____

____

____

New Neighborhood

I moved to Boston to a whole new world of big old houses on a neighborhood street. A girl who lived below me was a nurse and she found Christ. And there was another girl who lived next door. Her name was Barbara. I never told her I was a Christian. I just tried to love her and waited on Jesus to open the door.

One day she knocked on my kitchen door and said, "Ann." She was crying. "Ann, just tell me one thing. You are always so happy. What is it that makes you so happy?"

"Well, Barbara, I've been wanting to tell you. The most exciting thing in my life is that I chose to follow Jesus. No one makes me, I chose to. It was the most personal decision of my life and I have chosen to follow him because I know it pays. And because he loves me and love makes all the difference."

"Ann, how can I find him?"

And at the kitchen counter in my little apartment, Barbara, my neighbor, found him.

A month later she moved out and another girl moved in and I couldn't wait for my first night home. I ran over and knocked on her back door. "I just wondered. Do you go to church anywhere?"

"No, I'm not exactly the church type."

"Oh, I see. I didn't mean to be offensive. I understand. But I have a very exciting church and usually I'm out of town on Sundays, but I was wondering if some weekend when I'm in town if you would want to go with me?"

"Well, I guess so."

The next week she knocked on my door. "Is this one of your weekends at home? I just want to go to church with you."

And she did. But that wasn't when she found Christ. It was one night when I knocked on her door and sat at her kitchen table with her.

"Jesus Christ can make a difference in your life, Linda. He'll be your friend. He'll walk with you, he'll be your Lord, even as he is mine."

And in tears at a kitchen table she accepted him.

Two months ago she moved to Florida and now a

couple lives in her apartment. I'm so excited. I'm out to love them to Jesus. And I will. You watch, you wait, you'll see.

Give up? Never. My aim is victory. No matter how hard the road. I have a giant of a God and he and I in love can do it.

From *I'm Out to Change My World* by Ann Kiemel, © 1974 by Impact Books, Nashville, Tenn. Used by permission.

1 In a Bible dictionary, look up and write down the definition of the term "election."

2 Summarize what each of the following passages has to say about God's work in calling us:

1 THESSALONIANS 1:4

ROMANS 8:28-30

ROMANS 11:5, 7, 29

2 TIMOTHY 2:19

COLOSSIANS 3:12-17

EPHESIANS 1:4, 5

3 What does this doctrine mean to you?

 Map Study Date __________

1 The dots on the map of Greece below represent the sites of several early church communities. Find a Bible map of the time and label the following cities: Philippi, Thessalonica, Beroea, Athens, and Corinth.

2 Draw a line between each of the cities on this map together with arrows showing the direction in which Paul traveled on his second missionary journey.

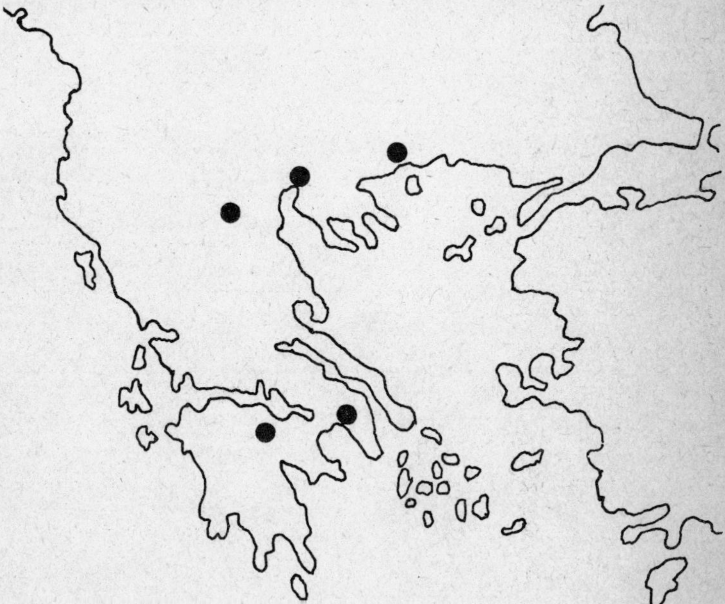

WEEK 3/ DAY 6 **Verse Glance** Date ____________
Examine 1 Thessalonians 2:13 carefully.

1 What is the subject of this verse?

____

____

2 How do you think Paul knew his words were inspired?

____

____

____

3 What kind of power does the Word possess?

____

____

____

4 What is the central message of this verse?

____

____

WEEK 3/ DAY 7 **Meditation** Date ____________

Read 1 Thessalonians 2:17—3:13, considering the meaning of each phrase.

1 What verse do I want to meditate on today?

2 What has God given me from this passage?

Notes

Questions

The Rewards of Being a Witness

1 Thessalonians 2:17—3:13

WEEK

4

Introduction

What greater reward can a soul winner receive than to see his converts grow in the Lord? Paul had heard reports that the Thessalonians were growing, and he wanted desperately to return to their city to see if the reports were true. Satan thwarted his plans, so he was not able to find out about his spiritual children until he sent Timothy to visit them.

Paul sent Timothy away at a time when he needed his young associate badly, but he was more concerned that his converts be strengthened than that he receive assistance. The news that Timothy brought back was a great comfort in the midst of Paul's continued distress and affliction.

We can learn much from the methods of follow-up detailed in this passage. Paul's faithfulness in prayer and personal attention were greatly blessed by God.

Outline

1 Thessalonians 2:17—3:13

D. Paul's concern for the church (2:17—3:10)
   1. Paul's attempts to come to the church (2:17, 18)
   2. Paul's reward is their faith (2:19, 20)
   3. Paul sends Timothy to the church (3:1-5)
      a. To strengthen them in their persecution (3:1-4)
      b. To check on their faith (3:5)
   4. Paul's assistant returned (3:6-8)
   5. Paul's joy with the church (3:9, 10)
      a. He has difficulty giving enough thanks to God (3:9)
      b. He longs to see them again (3:10)

E. Paul prays for the church (3:11-13)
   1. That God will send them back (3:11)
   2. That their love will grow (3:12)
   3. That they will stand true (3:13)

WEEK 4/ DAY 1 **Epistle Study** Date ____________
Review quickly 1 Thessalonians 2:17—3:10.

1 Check the type(s) of passage:
Doctrinal____ Instructional____ Personal____
Correctional____

2 Summarize what happened between Paul and the Thessalonian church.

____

____

____

3 What methods of follow-up did the apostle use with the church?

____

____

4 What results did this follow-up bring?

____

____

5 How do you think Paul could tell the difference between Satan's opposition and God closing a door?

____

____

6 What basic doctrinal truths can you glean from this passage?

____

____

____

7 What principles does God want to teach you?

____

____

____

WEEK 4/ DAY 2 **Psalm Glance** Date ____________
Examine Psalm 1.

1 Check the type of psalm:
Messianic or Prophetic____ Instructional____
Historical____ Nature____ Praise____ Prayer____

2 What is this psalm about?

____

____

3 Are any blessings promised?

____

____

4 What does this psalm say to you?

____

____

Imagine you are a member of the Thessalonian church during the first century. Write a short note responding to 1 Thessalonians 3:1-10.

Dear Paul,

____

____

____

____

____

____

____

____

____

WEEK 4/ DAY 4 Date ____________
Biography Study, Part 1

HISTORY
Summarize the major facts of Paul's life in chronological order (use the Ready-Reference section):

1 His conversion:

2 His early Christian life:

3 First missionary journey:

4 Second missionary journey:

5 Third missionary journey:

6 Trial and imprisonment at Rome:

APPLICATION
What does Paul's life teach you?

WEEK 4/ DAY 5 Date ___________

Biography Study, Part 2

BACKGROUND

Use the Ready-Reference section to study Paul's life further.

1 Meaning of his names:

____

2 His training:

____

____

3 His race, tribe, and parents:

____

4 His citizenship:

____

5 Place of birth:

____

CHARACTER

1 His basic temperament:

____

2 His character faults:

____

3 His good qualities:

____

4 His attitude toward God:

____

APPLICATION

What can you see of yourself in Paul?

____

____

Faith-Sized Requests

"Lord," prayed Jack, "I'd like to meet the fellow living next door in some casual way and begin to get acquainted with him. I'd like to begin today, and I believe You can arrange it for me. Thank You, Lord." Mary agreed with Jack in her prayer, and gave thanks with him.

The morning had scarcely turned to afternoon when the answer came. Their children got into a quarrel over a tricycle with the neighbor's children. Both fathers rushed to the scene. Jack took all the blame for his children, and put out his hand, "I'm Jack M., just moved in, glad to meet you." The first request had been answered. The first step had been taken.

The second step: "Lord, I'd like to know what that man is interested in, so we could become friends." The answer came within two days. He was interested in football.

The third step: "Lord, I need two complimentary football tickets, and could I have them by this weekend, please." The tickets came. The friendship grew.

The fourth step: "Lord, I'd like to invite this new friend to the Bible class I teach a few miles from here. Would You put it into his heart to accept when I ask him to go with me tonight?" He accepted. All the way over as they drove, they talked about football. All the way home they talked about Jesus Christ, and what it meant for Him to become one of us ... God became a Man.

The fifth step: "Lord, Mary and I would like to invite my friend and his wife to our home some evening this week and have a little talk and Bible reading together." The friends came, and they talked quietly together.

The sixth step. "Lord, next week when I ask them over again, will You prepare their hearts, so that they will be ready to accept You as their Savior? I believe this is the time to ask for this, and I thank You for all You'll be doing in the meantime to draw them to Yourself." When the next week came, the neighbors willingly and gladly accepted Jesus Christ.

WEEK 4/ DAY 6 **Verse Glance** Date ____________
Examine Hebrews 12:11.

1 What is the subject of this verse?

____

____

2 What light does the context give?

____

____

3 Why is discipline (even if punishment) important?

____

____

4 What does this verse say to you?

____

____

____

WEEK 4/ DAY 7 **Meditation** Date ____________
Read 1 Thessalonians 4:1-12, considering the meaning of each phrase.

1 Choose a verse to meditate on today. Rephrase it in your own words.

____

____

____

____

2 What has God taught you from this passage?

____

____

____

____

____

Notes

Questions

The Pure Life
1 THESSALONIANS 4:1-8

WEEK

5

Introduction

The Christians at Thessalonica had turned to God from idols. Idolatry in the year A.D. 50 often involved immorality. Worship in heathen temples often meant union with a temple "virgin." Because some of these Macedonian believers had such a background, the apostle's exhortation in this section is very much to the point.

Paul lays out the teachings on purity given by the authority of Christ. Sexual morality is not an optional part of Christianity. If we don't obey these teachings, we are rejecting not human teachers but God.

Each believer must know how to marry in holiness and honor. Strong personal desire for self-gratification is never acceptable before God. Paul makes it clear that lust is always wrong. We do well to examine the purity of our lives in light of this strong section of God's Word. Are we living a pure life?

Outline

1 Thessalonians 4:1-8

IV Social problems of the church (4:1-12)
- A. The problem of sexual immorality (4:1-8)
  - 1. How to please God sexually (4:1-5)
    - a. Live up to God's ideal (4:1, 2)
    - b. Keep clear of all sexual sin (4:3, 4)
    - c. Don't marry in lustful passion (4:5)
  - 2. How to know God's will in morality (4:6, 7)
    - a. Never take another's wife immorally (4:6a)
      - (1)The Lord will punish terribly for that (4:6b)
      - (2)We have told you this before (4:6c)
    - b. God has not caused us to be dirty-minded (4:7a)
    - c. God has called us to be holy and clean (4:7b)
  - 3. The consequences of disobeying these rules (4:8)
    - a. You will not be disobeying man (4:8a)
    - b. You will be disobeying God (4:8b)

WEEK 5/ DAY 1 **Grammar Study** Date ____________

Look up 1 Thessalonians 4:7

1 What is the subject of the sentence?

____

2 What is the subject doing?

____

3 List the qualities God desires in Christians.

____

____

4 What kind of behavior are you to avoid?

____

____

5 What kind of behavior should you practice?

____

____

WEEK 5/ DAY 2 **Epistle Study** Date ____________
Review quickly 1 Thessalonians 4:1-8.

1 Check the type(s) of passage:
Doctrinal____ Instructional____ Personal____
Correctional____

2 Summarize the basic content of the passage.

3 Does this passage condemn sexual relations in marriage?

4 How can you marry in holiness and honor?

5 Why is it important not to take another person's husband or wife?

6 What basic doctrinal truths can you glean from this passage?

7 What principles does God want you to learn?

1 Select a meaningful verse to memorize.

2 The verse you've selected:

____

3 Exact passage to be memorized:

____

____

____

4 Write the message of this verse in your own words.

____

____

____

5 Why do you want to memorize this passage?

____

____

6 Begin memorizing, word for word.

7 When you're ready, cover the verse above and test yourself by writing it here.

____

____

____

____

8 Review this verse during the rest of the week. This will help you to check your retention:

Review date _____ Perfect _____ Fair _______ Poor ______

Review date _____ Perfect _____ Fair _______ Poor ______

Review date _____ Perfect _____ Fair _______ Poor ______

Review date _____ Perfect _____ Fair _______ Poor ______

WEEK 5/ DAY 4 Date ___________

Five W's (Who, When, Where, What, Why)

Skim Genesis 39:1-23.

1 *Who* was involved?

____

2 *When* did this take place?

____

APPROXIMATE DATE

____

RELATIONSHIP TO SOME OTHER EVENT

____

____

3 *Where* did the action take place?

____

COUNTRY

____

GEOGRAPHY

____

BUILDINGS

4 *What* took place?

____

____

____

____

5 *Why* did this event take place?

____

____

____

____

6 What does God want to teach you from this passage?

____

____

____

____

WEEK 5/ DAY 5 **Law Study** Date ____________
Examine Leviticus 16:16-34.

1 What does this passage command to be done or not to be done?

____

____

2 At what group was this law aimed?

____

3 Would their basic need apply to you?

____

____

4 What is God's unchangeable principle behind this law?

____

____

____

____

5 Read Hebrews 9:9, 10; 13:4. What points are made in these verses?

____

____

____

6 What has God taught you for practical living from this passage?

____

____

____

WEEK 5/ DAY 6 **Teachings of Jesus** Date ____________

Read Matthew 5:27-32 carefully.

1 What does Jesus command?

____

____

____

2 What good qualities is he encouraging?

____

____

____

3 Why does he give this command?

____

____

____

4 Does Jesus really want people to do physical harm to themselves if they cannot keep from sinning?

____

What is he trying to communicate by this command?

____

____

____

5 What must your moral standard be according to this passage?

____

____

6 How can you apply these teachings?

____

____

____

WEEK 5/ DAY 7 **Proverbs Glance** Date ____________

Look up Proverbs 10:19-23.

1 What positive qualities are displayed?

____

____

2 What negative qualities are displayed?

____

____

3 What basic principle is God teaching?

____

____

____

4 How can you use this principle?

____

____

The Enemies of Sexual Happiness

Into a health clinic in San Francisco landed two thousand girls who had been enthralled by the flutes ... of a variety of pied pipers. These girls were asked if they had obtained even transitory pleasure from their sexual experiences. According to the advocates of sexual freedom, one would expect an enthusiastic affirmative. On the contrary, only a third of the girls reported "some pleasure." The other two thirds described their feelings as those of "doubt, guilt, shame, indifference, or definitely unpleasant."

It should ever be remembered that it is God who created sex urges in men and women, and God put His stamp of approval on marriage.... The restraints in God's Guidebook were never designed to diminish man's sexual enjoyment but rather to enable him to achieve maximal pleasure in this area. Pathetic indeed that many people are like cows who break through a fence surrounding their lush pasturage and then live on starvation rations in a desert of cactus.

Notes

Questions

How to Mind Your Own Business
1 THESSALONIANS 4:9-12

WEEK
6

Introduction

All of us would like to be financially independent. Often it is our desire for material possessions that causes us a lack of spiritual power. In this passage the apostle explains how we can reach satisfaction in the material world.

Personal satisfaction must begin with love for others. Self-love can never satisfy the longings of the heart. If you lead a quiet life and don't jump into everyone else's business, you will be satisfied. When you do your own work and bring in your own money, it will tend to bring a sense of accomplishment and well-being. Do these things and you will be respected by non-Christians and you won't be in any need.

If you follow the Apostle's instructions, when you are down financially, other Christians will come to your aid. You will also have less desire to possess things. Examine your own attitudes about work and finances while studying this passage.

Outline

1 Thessalonians 4:9-12

B. The problem of social morality (4:9-12)
   1. The need for pure brotherly love among believers (4:9, 10)
      a. Not much about this needed to be said (4:9a)
      b. God was already teaching them to love one another (4:9b)
      c. Their love was already strong toward other believers (4:10a)
      d. They were encouraged to love even more (4:10b)
   2. The kind of life they should lead (4:11)
      a. Live a quiet life (4:11a)
      b. Mind your own business (4:11b)
      c. Do your own work (4:11c)
   3. The results of this kind of life (4:12)
      a. Non-Christians will trust and respect you (4:12a)
      b. You will not need to depend on others to pay your bills (4:12b)

WEEK 6/ DAY 1 **Epistle Study** Date ____________
Review quickly 1 Thessalonians 4:9-12.

1 Check the type(s) of passage:
Doctrinal____ Instructional____ Personal____
Correctional____

2 Summarize the basic content of the passage.

3 What exhortations or commands are given?

4 How can a Christian lead a quiet life and mind his own business and still be an effective witness?

5 What blessings are promised in this passage?

6 What basic doctrinal truths can you glean from this passage?

7 What principles does God want you to learn?

WEEK 6/ DAY 2 **Observation** Date ____________
Examine 2 Thessalonians 3:10-12.

1 What is the main thing this passage teaches?

____

____

2 Why was it so important for everyone to work?

____

____

3 How would you guess these nonworkers were obtaining their food?

____

4 What is your attitude toward work?

____

____

____

WEEK 6/ DAY 3 **Verse Glance** Date ____________
Examine James 5:16.

1 What is the subject of this verse?

____

____

2 What light does the context give?

____

____

3 Why should we confess our faults to one another?

____

____

4 What does this verse say to you?

____

____

____

WEEK 6/ DAY 4 **Biography Study** Date ___________
Study Timothy's life.

BACKGROUND (see Ready-Reference section)

1 Meaning of his name:

____

2 His training:

____

3 His race, tribe, and parents:

____

CHARACTER

1 His basic temperament:

____

2 His spiritual condition:

____

HISTORY

Summarize the major facts of his life.

1 Conversion:

____

____

2 On Paul's second journey:

____

____

3 On third journey:

____

____

APPLICATION

What does his life teach you?

____

____

 Contrast Date __________

1 Summarize Ephesians 4:28, 29.

2 Summarize Colossians 4:5, 6.

3 Summarize 1 Thessalonians 4:12.

4 What obligation do Christians have toward non-Christians?

5 What obligations do Christians have to fellow Christians?

6 Does your speech have the effect Paul says it should have?

How can you improve it?

7 What has God taught you from these passages?

 Correspondence Date ____________

Imagine that the Apostle Paul is alive today. Write a note to him explaining how you plan to apply 1 Thessalonians 4:9-12.

Dear Paul,

WEEK 6/ DAY 7 **Meditation** Date ____________
Read 1 Thessalonians 4:13-18, considering the meaning of each phrase.

1 Choose a verse to meditate on today. Rephrase it in your own words.

____

____

____

____

2 What has God taught you from this passage?

____

____

____

____

____

Notes

Questions

Future Tense—
He's Coming Soon!
1 THESSALONIANS
4:13-18

WEEK

7

Introduction

To relieve fears concerning what happens to the dead, Paul explains what will happen when the Lord descends for his saints. When a believer dies, he goes to be with the Lord (2 Cor. 5:8). When Christ returns to take his people from the face of the earth, the dead in Christ will meet us in the air and together we shall be with the Lord forever.

There is much speculation as to when this event, called the "rapture," will take place. Many conservative scholars believe it will happen at the beginning of the seven-year tribulation period; this view is called the "pre-tribulation" theory. Another view holds to a "mid-tribulation" rapture. A third group believes that the church will be taken from the earth after this seven-year period; this is called the "post-tribulation" theory.

Outline
1 Thessalonians 4:13-18

V The doctrinal problems of the church (4:13—5:11)
- A. The problem of what happens to a Christian at death (4:13-18)
    - 1. The purpose of the passage (4:13a, 18)
        - a. So you will not be full of sorrow when a Christian dies (4:13b)
        - b. So that you will have a hope (4:13c)
        - c. So that you can comfort one another (4:18)
    - 2. The importance of Christ's resurrection (4:14)
        - a. We believe that Jesus was raised from the dead (4:14a)
        - b. We believe that when he returns we will again meet Christians who have died (4:14b)
    - 3. The events at the rapture (4:15-18)
        - a. The Christians who are alive at Christ's coming (4:15, 17)
            - (1)We will not rise ahead of those who are already dead (4:15)
            - (2)We shall be caught up together with the Lord (4:17a)
        - b. The sequence of events at the rapture (4:16, 17)
            - (1)The Lord himself will come down from heaven (4:16a)
            - (2)The dead believers will rise first to meet him (4:16b)
            - (3)Then living Christians will be caught up (4:17a)
            - (4)We will spend eternity with the Lord (4:17b)

Going Up!

The young executive yawned slightly as he entered the familiar lobby of the office building at the start of another routine day of business. He scarcely acknowledged the presence of the elevator dispatcher, who gestured to an open elevator and said "Going up." He certainly didn't imagine that the dispatcher's familiar call, "Going up," was prophetic and would be fulfilled at once!

Somewhere around the tenth floor he heard an earsplitting shout and the unmistakable sound of a trumpet blast overhead. And then he really began going up!

Before he could blink his eyes, or wonder if the others in the elevator had heard the strange sounds, the young executive was shooting up the elevator shaft. He seemed to take off like a rocket, going right through the top of the elevator and continuing right through the top of the building itself! He was careening upward through the bright morning sunshine and enjoying a completely euphoric feeling of well-being.

He was dumbfounded, but he was loving it! All around him he saw other people accelerating through the air, and they glowed white. They shined like silver against the blue sky. He suddenly realized that he too was "shining" in this peculiar way, and that his body had somehow been changed.

Before his mind could put it all together, his eyes looked upward and saw what was drawing him and all the others into the sky like a gigantic magnet.

There He was! Jesus Christ Himself!...

...He understood instantly that he was in the Rapture. He realized that he and the other believers around him in the air had suddenly become "like Jesus," seeing Him face-to-face and possessing their new resurrection bodies.

It was true! The promise was real and it was being fulfilled!

WEEK 7/ DAY 1 **Prophecy Study** Date ____________
Carefully examine 1 Thessalonians 4:13-18.

1 To whom is this prophecy given?

____

2 Why was this prophecy given?

____

____

3 What event is predicted?

____

____

____

4 What happens when Christ appears in the air?

____

____

____

5 Where will Christians go after this event?

____

____

6 What proof do we have that all this will take place?

____

____

____

7 What basic ideas is God teaching you?

____

____

____

 Contrast Date ____________

1 Summarize 2 Corinthians 5:8.

2 Summarize Philippians 1:22, 23.

3 Summarize 1 Thessalonians 4:13-15.

4 Where do the dead go?

5 What attitude should Christians have toward death?

6 What is your attitude toward death?

7 What has God taught you from these passages?

WEEK 7/ DAY 3 **Meditation** Date ____________

Read Matthew 24:29-44, considering the meaning of each phrase.

1 Choose a verse to meditate on today. Rephrase it in your own words.

____

____

____

____

2 What has God taught you from this passage?

____

____

____

____

____

Summarize the contents of Ezekiel chapters 38 and 39 below. If the passage contains a prophecy, write "P" at the right.

38:1-7

38:8-12

38:13

38:14-16

38:17-23

39:1-6

39:7, 8

39:9, 10

39:11-16

39:17-21

39:22-24

39:25-29

WEEK 7/ DAY 5 **Teachings of Jesus** Date ____________

Read Matthew 24:45-51 carefully.

1 Summarize the story Jesus tells.

____

____

2 What does the story teach?

____

____

3 What are the rewards for the faithful?

____

____

____

4 What is the punishment for the unfaithful?

____

____

____

5 Why do you think Jesus used this type of example?

____

____

____

6 What underlying principle is Jesus teaching?

____

____

____

7 How can you apply these teachings?

____

____

____

WEEK 7/ DAY 6 **Verse Glance** Date ___________
Examine 1 John 5:13.

1 What is this verse about?

____

____

2 What does it mean to believe in the name of the Son of God?

____

____

3 What does the word *know* tell you?

____

____

4 What does this verse say personally to you?

____

____

WEEK 7/ DAY 7 **Meditation** Date __________

Read 1 Thessalonians 5:1-11 carefully, considering the meaning of each phrase.

1 Choose a verse to meditate on today. Rephrase it in your own words.

2 What has God taught you from this passage?

Notes

Questions

Wanted:
Dead or Alive
1 THESSALONIANS 5:1-11

WEEK

8

Introduction

In this section Paul talks about the prophetic "day of the Lord." The term is generally used in Scripture to indicate God's judgment. Some feel that this prophetic "day" (or period of time) starts when the tribulation period begins. Others suggest that it starts at the end of the tribulation, when the second coming will take place and Christ will defeat his foes at Armageddon.

Peter tells us that in the last days people will say, "So Jesus promised to come back, did he? Then where is he? He'll never come back!" (2 Peter 3:4). Peter goes on to say, "But don't forget this, dear friends, that a day or a thousand years from now is like tomorrow to the Lord.... The day of the Lord is surely coming."

Paul also makes it plain that the Lord will come suddenly, but that it need not take Christians by surprise. Whether we are dead or alive, when that day begins, we will go to live with him forever.

Outline

1 Thessalonians 5:1-11

B. The problem concerning the second coming (5:1-11)
   1. Your knowledge of when Christ will come (5:1-3)
      a. No one needs to tell you these things (5:1)
      b. You know the Lord will come like a thief in the night (5:2)
      c. You know disaster will fall suddenly (5:3)
   2. Your response to Christ's coming (5:4-8)
      a. You won't be surprised when the Lord comes (5:4)
      b. You are of the light, so be on your guard (5:5, 6)
      c. You are not of the night, so keep sober (5:7, 8)
   3. Your assurance of being taken at Christ's coming (5:9, 10)
      a. God has not chosen to pour his anger upon us (5:9)
      b. Jesus died for us so that we might live with him forever (5:10)
   4. Your work now—encourage and build each other up (5:11)

WEEK 8/ DAY 1 **Verse Glance** Date ____________
Examine 1 Thessalonians 5:8.

1 What is the subject of this verse?

____

____

2 What does the context tell you?

____

____

3 In practical terms, what does this verse tell Christians to do?

____

____

4 What does this verse say to you?

____

____

The Main Event

When Jesus returns the second time it will be as a lion to judge those who rejected the free gift of salvation from sin. Man will have completely demonstrated his worthiness of judgment.

According to Zechariah, "all nations will be gathered against Jerusalem to battle." The Jews who live in the area will be on the verge of annihilation when God gives them supernatural strength to fight. Then the Lord will go forth to fight for them and save them.

Jesus' feet will first touch the earth where they left the earth, on the Mount of Olives. The mountain will split in two with a great earthquake the instant that Jesus' foot touches it. The giant crevice which results will run east and west through the center of the mountain. It will go east to the north tip of the Dead Sea and west to the Mediterranean Sea (Zechariah 14).

 Prophecy Study Date ____________

Carefully examine 1 Thessalonians 5:1-4.

1 To whom is this prophecy given?

____

2 Why do you think this prophecy was given?

____

____

3 What event is predicted?

____

____

____

4 When will this event take place?

____

____

____

5 What does the prophetic term "that day" or "the day of the Lord" mean? (See Ready-Reference section.)

____

____

____

6 How can we be prepared for the Lord's coming?

____

____

____

7 What principle is God teaching?

____

____

____

WEEK 8/ DAY 3 **Epistle Study** Date ____________
Review quickly 1 Thessalonians 5:4-11.

1 Check the type(s) of passage:
Doctrinal ____ Instructional ____ Personal ____
Correctional ____

2 Summarize the basic content of the passage.

____

____

____

____

3 List all the symbolism used to describe the righteous.

____

____

4 List all the symbolism used to describe the unrighteous.

____

____

5 What exhortation or commands are given?

____

____

____

6 What basic doctrinal truths can you glean from this passage?

____

____

____

7 What does God want you to learn?

____

____

____

WEEK 8/ DAY 4 **Meditation** Date ____________

Read Ephesians 6:10-20 carefully, considering the meaning of each phrase.

1 Choose a verse to meditate on today. Rephrase it in your own words.

____

____

____

____

2 What has God taught you from this passage?

____

____

____

____

____

WEEK 8/ DAY 5 **Psalm Glance** Date ____________

Examine Psalm 23.

1 Check the type of psalm:
Messianic or Prophetic ____ Instructional ____
Historical ____ Nature ____ Praise ____ Prayer ____

2 What is this psalm about?

____

____

3 Are any blessings promised?

____

____

4 What does this psalm say to you?

____

____

WEEK 8/ DAY 6 **Epistle Study** Date ____________
Read 1 Corinthians 15:50-58.

1 Check the type(s) of passage:
Doctrinal ____ Instructional ____ Personal ____
Correctional ____

2 Summarize the basic content of the passage.

____

____

____

3 What happens to our bodies at the rapture?

____

____

4 Why is sin called a sting?

____

____

____

5 What basic doctrinal truths can you glean from this passage?

____

____

____

6 What exhortations or commands are given?

____

____

____

7 What does God want you to learn?

____

____

____

Israel in Agony

He was in the Kidron Valley, moving slowly, terrified, from tree to tree and rock to rock. There were machine-gun bullets hitting all around him. Heavy shells hit the hills in front. The Temple, only half a mile behind his present position, was a wall of flames that lit the night. Horrible explosions racked the city of Jerusalem.

"I'm coming, Lord," was all he could think of.

Suddenly there was a tremendous wrenching roar from the Mount of Olives ahead of him. The world seemed to crunch in two at that impossible crashing sound. His ears went dead and his head was wracked through with terrible pain.

But his eyes were working and he looked up, half in terror, half in hope.

And there before him, in majesty and splendor, stood, of all people ... Jesus Christ!

WEEK 8/ DAY 7 **Meditation** Date ___________

Read 1 Thessalonians 5:12-28, considering the meaning of each phrase.

1 Choose a verse to meditate on today. Rephrase it in your own words.

____

____

____

____

2 What has God taught you from this passage?

____

____

____

____

____

Notes

Questions

Present Tense—
Live the Christian
Life with Power
1 THESSALONIANS
5:12-28

WEEK
9

Introduction

In his closing comments in the first Thessalonian letter, Paul gives several practical exhortations for living the Christian life.

He encourages the Thessalonians to respond properly to the chain-of-command. They are to think highly of the spiritual leaders who labor in their church. They are to live in peace with one another and warn the undisciplined. They are to help one another, offer encouragement, and be patient to all. They are not to pay back evil for evil.

The apostle then proceeds to encourage his spiritual children to have the proper attitude moment by moment. They are to keep on praying about things, and be thankful whatever happens.

This is a practical section of Scripture from which we can learn a lot. Examine it carefully during the next week.

Outline

1 Thessalonians 5:12-28

VI Important exhortations (5:12-28)

- A. Your attitude toward the officers in the church (5:12, 13)
  1. Honor those who work hard (5:12)
  2. Give them your wholehearted love (5:13)
- B. Your behavior toward others (5:14-18)
  1. Warn those who are lazy (5:14a)
  2. Comfort those who are frightened (5:14b)
  3. Take care of the weak (5:14c)
  4. Be patient with everyone (5:14d)
  5. Never pay back evil for evil (5:15)
  6. Always be joyful (5:16)
  7. Always keep on praying (5:17)
  8. Always be thankful (5:18)
- C. Your spiritual behavior (5:19-22)
  1. Don't smother the Holy Spirit (5:19)
  2. Don't scoff at those who prophesy but test everything that is said (5:20, 21)
  3. Keep away from every kind of evil (5:22)

VII Conclusion (5:23-28)

- A. Paul's prayer for the church (5:23)
- B. Paul's final instructions and closing (5:24-28)

WEEK 9/ DAY 1 **Verse Glance** Date ____________
Examine Philippians 2:3, 4.

1 What is the subject of these verses?

____

2 List the kinds of negative qualities Christians are not to exhibit.

____

____

3 In practical terms, what are these verses telling you to do?

____

____

4 How can you apply these truths?

____

____

The Process of Making Disciples

Making disciples takes time. It cannot be done through a series of lectures and a training seminar in the church, nor can it be done by reading a book. It cannot be rushed. One of the dominant characteristics of our modern culture is our ability and desire to mass-produce. We mass-produce everything—cars, appliances, furniture, pots and pans, and household gadgets.... It is so easy to take this "mass-produced mentality" and apply it to disciple-making. It cannot be done. Disciples are made, but not mass-produced. Each one is molded and fashioned individually by the Spirit of God.

How long it takes is a matter of conjecture and varies from person to person, depending to a large degree on where they are when they begin the training process. But one thing is certain; it does take time. The Lord Jesus began with twelve monotheistic, God-fearing men, who came from reasonably good homes. He devoted himself full time to their training and development. He was a Master at the art of training, and yet it took Him three full years. We can hardly hope to do it in less.

From *Disciples Are Made–Not Born* by Walter A. Henrichsen, © 1974 by Victor Books, Wheaton, Ill. Used by permission.

WEEK 9/ DAY 2 **Epistle Study** Date ____________
Review quickly 1 Thessalonians 5:12-18.

1 Check the type(s) of passage:
Doctrinal ____ Instructional ____ Personal ____
Correctional ____

2 Summarize the content of this passage.

____

____

____

3 How are Christians to respond toward their spiritual leaders?

____

____

4 Why?

____

____

____

5 What basic doctrinal truths can you glean from this passage?

____

____

____

6 What exhortations or commands are given?

____

____

____

7 What does God want you to learn?

____

____

____

 Epistle Study Date ____________
Review 1 Thessalonians 5:19-28 carefully.

1 Check the type(s) of passage:
Doctrinal ___ Instructional ___ Personal ___
Correctional ___

2 Summarize the content of this passage.

____

____

____

3 List the things Christians are to do.

____

____

____

4 List the things Christians are not to do.

____

____

____

5 What does verse 24 tell you about God and his work in you?

____

____

____

6 What basic doctrinal truths can you glean from this passage?

____

____

7 What does God want you to learn?

____

____

____

 Symbolism Study Date ____________

1 The apostle uses a number of symbolic terms in 1 Thessalonians. Summarize what each of these terms is meant to describe.

"MOTHER" (2:7)

"FATHER" (2:11)

"TROPHY" (2:20)

"LITTLE CRACKS" (3:10)

"THIEF" (5:2)

"BIRTH PAINS" (5:3)

"LIGHT AND DAY" (5:5)

"DARKNESS AND NIGHT" (5:5)

"ARMOR" (5:8)

"HELMET" (5:8)

2 Why do you think biblical writers use so much symbolism?

3 List some of the symbolic titles of Christ.

WEEK 9/ DAY 5 **Verse Glance** Date ____________
Examine Psalm 119:165

1 What is the subject of this verse?

____

____

2 What does "love your laws" imply?

____

____

3 How all-inclusive are the words "do not stumble"?

____

____

4 How can you apply this verse?

____

____

 Correspondence Date ____________

Write a letter to a close friend explaining some of the important doctrines in 1 Thessalonians.

WEEK 9/ DAY 7 **Meditation** Date ____________

Read 2 Thessalonians 1:1-12, considering the meaning of each phrase.

1 Choose a verse to meditate on today. Rephrase it in your own words.

____

____

____

____

2 What has God taught you from this passage?

____

____

____

____

____

Notes

Questions

Persecution? Here's What to Expect
2 THESSALONIANS 1:1-12

WEEK

10

Introduction

Persecution. No one really looks forward to it. It's no fun to have your faith tried by unbelievers. But sooner or later we will all face persecution of some type.

In 2 Thessalonians 1, Paul praises these new Christians for their solid stand under heavy persecution. He also tells them what to expect: God repays those who afflict Christians, and Christ will give relief to all believers everywhere when he returns with his mighty angels.

What a tremendous expectation all Christians have: Jesus is coming back for us. And when he does, Christ will receive glory and praise from us. Make certain you are worthy of his calling.

Outline

2 Thessalonians 1:1-12

I Introduction of the letter (1:1, 2)

II What to expect in persecution (1:3-12)

- A. Paul is thankful for their growth (1:3, 4)
  1. We rejoice at your growing love for each other (1:3)
  2. We tell others of your complete faith in spite of your crushing troubles (1:4)
- B. Paul outlines the purpose of persecution (1:5, 6)
  1. Your sufferings are making you ready for God's kingdom (1:5)
  2. God prepares judgment for those who hurt you (1:6)
- C. Paul expects certain results from this persecution (1:7-10)
  1. God will give you rest when the Lord returns (1:7)
  2. God will bring judgment on non-Christians (1:8, 9)
     - a. Punished in everlasting hell (1:8, 9a)
     - b. Forever separated from God (1:9b)
  3. God will do all this when Christ returns (1:10)
- D. Paul's prayer for the church's fulfillment (1:11, 12)
  1. That God will make you good children (1:11)
  2. That everyone will praise the Lord because of you (1:12)

WEEK 10/ DAY 1 Date ___________

Book Study, Part, 1

Skim 2 Thessalonians quickly.

BACKGROUND (use Ready-Reference section if necessary)

1 Who is the writer?

____

____

HIS OCCUPATION

____

APPROXIMATE AGE

____

PERSONALITY TRAITS

2 Where was the book written?

____

3 Where was it sent?

____

4 When was it written?

____

5 Why was it written?

____

____

THEME

1 What ideas stand out at your first reading?

____

____

____

2 Summarize the contents of the book.

____

____

____

3 What verses stand out?

____

WEEK 10/ DAY 2 Date ___________

Book Study, Part 2

Read 2 Thessalonians quickly again.

SPECIAL CHARACTERISTICS

1 What are some of the important teachings of this book?

____

____

____

2 What personal information does the author give?

____

____

____

OUTLINE SUMMARY

Draft a simple outline of the main points contained in the book.

____

____

____

____

____

____

____

____

____

____

APPLICATION

What subjects does this book deal with that you need?

____

____

____

WEEK 10/ DAY 3 **Epistle Study** Date ____________
Review 2 Thessalonians 1:1-6 carefully.

1 Check the type(s) of passage:
Doctrinal ____ Instructional ____ Personal ____
Correctional ____

2 Summarize the content of this passage.

____

____

____

____

3 How do your sufferings make you ready for God's kingdom?

____

____

____

4 According to the context, who will the judgment be against?

____

____

5 When will God bring this judgment?

____

____

6 What doctrinal truths can you glean from this passage?

____

____

____

7 What does God want you to learn?

____

____

____

WEEK 10/ DAY 4 **Epistle Study** Date ___________
Review 2 Thessalonians 1:6-12 carefully.

1 Check the type(s) of passage:
Doctrinal ____ Instructional ____ Personal ____
Correctional ____

2 Summarize the content of this passage.

____

____

____

3 When will Christians get relief from persecution?

____

____

4 What will Christians do when Christ returns?

____

____

5 List the things Paul prays for the Thessalonians.

____

____

____

____

6 What basic doctrinal truths can you glean from this passage?

____

____

____

7 What does God want you to learn?

____

____

____

WEEK 10/ DAY 5 Date ___________

Paragraph Glance

Summarize the contents of 2 Thessalonians below.

REFERENCES	SUMMARY
1:1, 2	
1:3-6	
1:7-10	
1:11, 12	
2:1-3a	
2:3b-6	
2:7-14	
2:15, 16	
3:1-5	
3:6-10	
3:11-16	
3:17, 18	

Broken, But Not Bowed

One young Christian was summoned to the DS (Secret Police) every night for six months for nightly beatings. By various means they tried to get him to promise to tell everything that happened in the congregation. He refused....

The same methods were used on many other young Christians throughout the country. Fervent Christians and active members were especially sought after by the DS. Many were not able to hold out, and bowed to the will of the authorities perhaps in order to remain in the congregation....

The communists knew an outward attack on the churches would unite and strengthen the believers, as it has done down through Christian history. So they decided to destroy or control it from within. To this day the communist tactic is to close some churches and install their own men in those that remain open.

 Contrast Date ____________

1 Summarize 2 Thes. 1:9.

2 Summarize Rev. 20:15.

3 Summarize Mark 9:47-49.

4 Summarize Matt. 25:41.

5 For whom was hell created?

6 Who goes to hell?

7 How is hell described?

8 What has God taught you from these passages?

Heartbreak Hotel

When the door slammed and the key turned in that rusty iron lock, a feeling of utter loneliness swept over me. I lay down on that cold cement slab in my 6 x 6 prison. The smell of human excrement burned my nostrils. A rat, large as a small cat, scampered across the slab beside me. The walls and floors and ceilings were caked with filth. Bars covered a tiny window high above the door. I was cold and hungry; my body ached....

My hunger for spiritual food soon outdid my hunger for a steak. Now I wanted to know about the part of me that will never die. Now I wanted to talk about God and Christ and the church. But in Heartbreak solitary confinement there was no pastor, no Sunday school teacher, no Bible, no hymnbook, no community of believers to guide and sustain me. I had completely neglected the spiritual dimension of my life. It took prison to show me how empty life is without God, and so I had to go back in my memory to those Sunday School days in the Nogales Avenue Baptist Church, Tulsa, Oklahoma. If I couldn't have a Bible and a hymnbook, I would try to rebuild them in my mind.

WEEK 10/ DAY 7 **Meditation** Date ____________

Read 2 Thessalonians 2:1-12, considering the meaning of each phrase.

1 Choose a verse to meditate on today. Rephrase it in your own words.

____

____

____

____

2 What has God taught you from this passage?

____

____

____

____

Notes

Questions

The Man of Lawlessness
2 THESSALONIANS 2:1-12

WEEK

11

Introduction

Evidently the Thessalonian believers had been disturbed by teachers who claimed that the Lord had already returned. Paul makes it plain that the coming of our Lord will not take place until a time of general apostasy begins. He reminds the Thessalonians that Christ will not come until this great "falling away." They should not believe anyone who teaches a different message.

The man of lawlessness, who is the Antichrist, is being held back from appearing by a restrainer. This restrainer is referred to both as a force and as a person. For this reason some scholars feel that the force is law and order and the "he" is a government head. Others believe that the force is the presence of Christians and that the "he" is the Holy Spirit. Whatever or whoever the restrainer is, when there is no more restraint, the man of sin will enter the scene and deceive many. Study this passage carefully so that you will know what the future holds.

Outline

2 Thessalonians 2:1-12

III An explanation of future events (2:1-12)
- A. The rumors are corrected about the Lord's coming (2:1-3a)
- B. Two things must happen before the Lord returns (2:3b-4)
  1. There will be a time of great rebellion (2:3b)
  2. The man of rebellion will come (2:3c, 4)
     - a. He will defy every god there is (2:4a)
     - b. He will sit in the temple and claim to be God (2:4b)
- C. Remember we told you this before (2:5)
- D. The restraining force (2:6, 7)
  1. You know what is keeping him from coming (2:6)
  2. He can't come until the restrainer steps out of the way (2:7)
- E. The end of the Antichrist (2:8)
- F. The works of the Antichrist (2:9)
- G. The people fooled by the Antichrist (2:10-12)

WEEK 11/ DAY 1 Date ___________

Prophecy Glance

Summarize the contents of Zechariah 14 listed below. If a paragraph contains a prophecy, write "P" at the right.

REFERENCE	SUMMARY
14:1, 2	
14:3-5	
14:6-8	
14:9-11	
14:12	
14:13-15	
14:16-19	
14:20, 21	

What is the main thing this passage predicts?

____

The Antichrist

He is a political leader of great acumen—virtually a sorcerer. He is engaging and appealing. He captures the loyalty of what is left of the world after the rapture, and he becomes a kind of inverse messiah. The world trusts him with its problems, and he certainly succeeds in putting it out of its misery.

He is an egomaniac to make Hitler, Napoleon, and all the Caesars fade into soft-spoken modesty. He steadily gathers power and influence through his public relations man, the False Prophet, and he finally proclaims himself—not king nor president nor world ruler—but God Almighty.

He does demonstrate seemingly supernatural powers, but they are not from above. The best that can be said of him is "the devil made him do it."

Modesty is not his long suit. He is fanatically sold on himself and his abilities. He is a man of tremendous energy and action; a diplomat and a peacemaker, a messiah and a field marshal.

WEEK 11/ DAY 2 **Prophecy Study** Date ____________

Carefully examine 2 Thessalonians 2:1-6.

1 To whom is the prophecy given?

2 Why do you think this prophecy was uttered?

3 What events are predicted?

4 How does the passage describe the man of lawlessness?

5 What will this man do?

6 What assurances did Paul give that these things would come true?

7 What basic truth is God teaching you?

WEEK 11/ DAY 3 **Prophecy Study** Date ___________

Carefully examine 2 Thessalonians 2:7-12.

1 To whom is the prophecy given?

2 Why do you think this prophecy was given?

3 What events are predicted?

4 How does this passage describe the man of rebellion?

5 What will cause people to believe in this lawless one?

6 Has any part of this prophecy been fulfilled?

7 What basic truth is God teaching you?

WEEK 11/ DAY 4 **Verse Glance** Date ____________
Examine John 3:18, 19.

1 What are these verses about?

____

____

2 What causes a person to be judged?

____

____

3 Why do you think people love darkness and evil deeds so much?

____

____

4 How can you apply these verses?

____

____

WEEK 11/ DAY 5 **Observation** Date ____________
Read Revelation 13:1-8.

1 The Dragon is Satan. The Creature is the Antichrist. Why will people worship the Creature?

____

____

2 How does the Creature behave?

____

____

3 What is the relationship between the Dragon and the Creature?

____

____

4 What has God taught you?

____

____

WEEK 11/ DAY 6 **Prophecy Study** Date ____________
Carefully examine Mark 13:14-23.

1 To whom is the prophecy given?

2 Why do you think this prophecy was given?

3 What events are predicted?

4 What will happen when the "horrible thing" stands in the Temple? (See Daniel 9:27; 11:31; 12:11.)

5 Do you think any Christians will be on earth at this time?

6 How will Satan try to mislead the elect?

7 What principles is God teaching you?

WEEK 11/ DAY 7 **Meditation** Date ____________

Read 2 Thessalonians 2:13—3:5, considering the meaning of each phrase.

1 Choose a verse to meditate on today. Rephrase it in your own words.

____

____

____

____

2 What has God taught you from this passage?

____

____

____

____

____

Notes

Questions

The Growth Experience

2 THESSALONIANS 2:13—3:5

WEEK

12

Introduction

Growth is work. Every chance we get, we want to quit the process because it takes so much effort. In this passage Paul encourages his spiritual children to grow in the faith in a number of different ways.

He explains some of the doctrines of salvation. He touches on being "called." He encourages the process of growing by telling these believers to stand firm with the truth they have been taught.

Paul then asks for prayer for his own ministry, that the Word of God may also spread and the faith might grow in the world. Paul has every confidence in the Thessalonians that they will continue to grow and be faithful to Christ. As you examine this doctrinal section examine your own personal calling to Christ.

Outline

2 Thessalonians 2:13–3:5

IV An encouragement of faith (2:13—3:5)
- A. Paul gives thanks for the Thessalonian believers (2:13, 14)
  1. God chose you from the very beginning for salvation (2:13)
  2. God called you to share in our Lord's glory (2:14)
- B. Paul encourages them to stand firm (2:15)
- C. Paul's prayer for the Thessalonian believers (2:16, 17)
- D. Paul requests prayer (3:1, 2)
  1. That the Lord's message will spread rapidly (3:1)
  2. That we will be saved from evil men (3:2)
- E. Paul encourages them to trust the Lord (3:3-5)
  1. The Lord will guard you from satanic attacks (3:3)
  2. We trust you will put into practice the Good News (3:4)
  3. May God give you a deeper love and patience (3:5)

WEEK 12/ DAY 1 **Biography Study** Date ____________

Study the life of Silas.

BACKGROUND (see Ready-Reference section)

1 Meaning of his name:

____

2 His preaching and spiritual gift:

____

CHARACTER

Summarize what you know of his character.

____

____

HISTORY

Summarize the major facts of his life:

1 How first introduced:

____

____

2 Imprisoned at Philippi:

____

____

3 Continues on with Paul:

____

____

4 Later ministry with Peter:

____

____

APPLICATION

What does his life teach you?

____

____

____

WEEK 12/ DAY 2 **Epistle Study** Date ____________
Review 2 Thessalonians 2:13-17 carefully.

1 Check the type(s) of passage:
Doctrinal ____ Instructional ____ Personal ____
Correctional ____

2 Summarize the content of this passage.

____

____

____

____

3 What does it mean to be "chosen"?

____

____

4 What are the things a chosen person does?

____

____

5 Why did God call us?

____

____

____

6 What doctrinal truths can you glean from this passage?

____

____

____

____

7 What does God want you to learn?

____

____

____

 Epistle Study Date ____________

Review 2 Thessalonians 3:1-5 thoughtfully.

1 Check the type(s) of passage:
Doctrinal ____ Instructional ____ Personal ____
Correctional ____

2 Summarize the basic content of this passage.

3 What type of prayer did Paul request?

4 How did the apostle expect to be guarded from satanic attacks?

5 How did the apostle want the Thessalonians to grow?

6 What doctrinal truths can you glean from this passage?

7 What does God want you to learn?

A New Plan

I realized that the only *real* time there is, or ever has been in which to live and act, is the now—the present moment. No decision, no birth, no death, nothing ever happened in a future or a past moment, only in a present one. And I had filled so many of the present moments of my life with the unreality of the past or future. The blinding introspection in which I had spent so much time had again and again blurred the intensity of my attention from seeing the *actual* opportunities and relationships which stood waiting before my eyes. I had marched into the future looking straight ahead—passing by the unconsciously searching eyes of those people beside the road which I was traveling.

This simple change of the focus of my attention to the immediate events of the moment as the important events—from God's perspective—made me realize that all of my background and training were not a kind of "practicing" preparing me for some big public Christian position sometime in the future. I now began to see that all my past was training me for the events and encounters of *this day*, however insignificant this day may seem from my perspective. Each day, each relationship, in my business life began to take on new importance. God might have something new to do in *this* relationship. I saw in the Scriptures that the days on which Christ was born, crucified, and rose from the dead did *not* seem important *as they were happening* even to most of the people present, but *only* to those who saw the events of those days from God's perspective. I began to realize that I could easily miss out on the things God may be doing in *this* day—the seeds He is planting, the new visions of renewal, the despair He wants to heal, the hope He wants to fulfill in a life—unless I began to see the possibilities of His healing action all around me along the pathways He will send me this hour.

WEEK 12/ DAY 4 **Verse Glance** Date ____________

Look at 1 Thessalonians 3:5.

1 What is this verse about?

____

____

2 What are the qualities we should have?

____

____

3 If you have patience, how will that quality reveal itself?

____

____

4 What does this verse say to you?

____

____

1 Select a meaningful verse to memorize.

2 Verse:

____

3 Write out passage to be memorized.

____

____

____

____

4 Begin memorizing, word for word.

5 When ready, check the verse you've learned by rewriting it here.

____

____

____

____

WEEK 12/ DAY 6 **Grammar Study** Date ____________
Look up 2 Thessalonians 3:1.

1 What is the subject of the first sentence?

____

2 What is the subject to do?

____

3 List the nouns in the second sentence.

____

4 List the action verbs in the second sentence.

____

5 What two things is this verse telling Christians to do?

____

____

____

WEEK 12/ DAY 7 **Meditation** Date ____________
Read 2 Thessalonians 3:6-18, considering the meaning of each phrase.

1 Choose a verse to meditate on today. Rephrase it in your own words.

____

____

____

____

2 What has God taught you from this passage?

____

____

____

____

____

Notes

Questions

The Disciplined Life
2 THESSALONIANS 3:6-18

WEEK

13

Introduction

Discipline is one of the most important qualities needed for success. Most people, however, have difficulty in disciplining their life-style. This section will help you organize both your personal and spiritual life.

Paul is well aware of what will happen if a person doesn't work. With extra time on his hands he will become a gossip and cause dissension among the saints. Paul gives strong exhortations to avoid those who live unruly, undisciplined lives. The Thessalonians are commanded to put such individuals to shame by not associating with them. The Apostle points to his own self-controlled behavior as a model. He worked long hours and paid for whatever food he received. Everyone who is not now working is commanded to quiet down and start working.

This passage is a good touchstone for twentieth-century Christians to use to examine not only their work habits, but their daily life discipline.

Outline
2 Thessalonians 3:6-18

V The problem of dealing with lazy Christians (3:6-16)
  A. How to handle the loafer (3:6-13)
    1. Stay away from lazy Christians (3:6)
    2. Follow our example (3:7-9)
      a. You never saw us loafing (3:7)
      b. We never accepted food without buying it (3:8a)
      c. We worked hard not to be a burden (3:8b)
      d. We had the right to ask you to feed us but we wanted to give you a good example (3:9)
    3. A clear-cut rule for the loafer (3:10)
    4. We hear of the problems (3:11)
    5. Our commands to all those in the church (3:12, 13)
  B. How to handle those who are disobedient (3:14-16)
    1. Take note and stay away from the disobedient (3:14)
    2. Don't think of him as an enemy (3:15a)
    3. Think of him as a brother who needs to be warned (3:15b)
    4. May the Lord give you peace in the matter (3:16)

VI Closing words (3:17, 18)
  A. Paul's greeting and authentication (3:17)
  B. Paul's benediction (3:18)

WEEK 13/ DAY 1 **Verse Glance** Date ___________
Examine 2 Thessalonians 3:6.

1 What is this verse about?

____

____

2 How can you avoid loafing Christians?

____

____

3 What example had the church received?

____

____

4 What does this verse say to you?

____

____

 Map Study Date ____________

The map of the Mediterranean area below shows the provinces of the Roman empire at approximately the time Paul wrote the Thessalonian epistles. Using a New Testament Bible map, label the following provinces: Italy, Achaia, Macedonia, Lycia, Galatia, Cappadocia, Syria, Pamphylia, Cilicia, and Thrace.

WEEK 13/ DAY 3 **Epistle Study** Date ____________
Quickly examine 2 Thessalonians 3:6-9.

1 Check the type(s) of passage:
Doctrinal ____ Instructional ____ Personal ____
Correctional ____

2 Summarize the content of this passage.

____

____

____

3 What kind of example did the apostles set?

____

____

____

4 Are you a disciplined person?

____

____

5 What exhortations or commands are given?

____

____

____

6 What doctrinal truths can you glean from this passage?

____

____

____

____

7 What principles does God want you to learn?

____

____

____

WEEK 13/ DAY 4 **Epistle Study** Date ___________
Quickly examine 2 Thessalonians 3:10-18.

1 Check the type(s) of passage:
Doctrinal ____ Instructional ____ Personal ____
Correctional ____

2 Summarize the content of this passage.

____

____

____

____

3 Why is it important that everyone live a disciplined life?

____

____

4 What is the connection between idleness and gossip?

____

____

5 What exhortations or commands are given?

____

____

____

6 What doctrinal truths can you glean from this passage?

____

____

____

____

7 What principles does God want you to learn?

____

____

____

List all the facts you can find about the church at Thessalonica and its members. Use both books and all your previous studies (check Ready-Reference section):

WEEK 13/ DAY 6 **Proverbs Glance** Date ____________
Look closely at Proverbs 6:6-11.

1 What positive qualities does the ant possess?

____

____

2 What negative qualities does the lazy man possess?

____

____

3 What basic principle is God teaching in this passage?

____

____

4 How can you benefit from this principle?

____

____

WEEK 13/ DAY 7 **Summary Study** Date ____________

Quickly skim both 1 and 2 Thessalonians.

1 Summarize the basic content of 1 Thessalonians.

2 Summarize the basic content of 2 Thessalonians.

3 What new doctrinal truths have you learned while studying the Thessalonian epistles?

4 Which verses had special meaning to you?

5 What can you share with others?

Notes

Questions

APPLICATION SUMMARY

1 Bad habits you need to break:

2 Bad attitudes that must go:

3 Godly habits you want to develop:

4 Godly attitudes you want to develop: